MATTESON PUBLIC LIBRARY

W9-AJD-125

DATE DUE

2/08

BENJAMIN BANNEKER

Mathematician and Stargazer

ROSE BLUE AND CORINNE J. NADEN

A GATEWAY BIOGRAPHY

The Millbrook Press

Brookfield, Connecticut

Cover photographs courtesy of Smithsonian Institution and Photographs and Prints Division, Schomberg Center for Research in Black Culture, The New York Public Library, Astor, Lenox and Tilden Foundations

Photographs courtesy of Photographs and Prints Division, Schomberg Center for Research in Black Culture, The New York Public Library, Astor, Lenox and Tilden Foundations: p. 4;© Corbis-Bettmann:pp.7, 12, 20; Lambert/Archive Photos: p. 11; © 2000 Jay Mallin: pp. 14, 40, 41; Maryland State Archives Special Collections: p. 16; Smithsonian Institution: pp. 22, 27; © Corbis: p. 24; Library of Congress: pp. 26, 31; North Wind Picture Archives: p. 28; The Granger Collection, New York: p. 32, 35; © U.S. Postal Service: p. 39

Library of Congress Cataloginig-in-Publication Data
Blue, Rose
Benjamin Banneker: mathematician and stargazer / Rose Blue and Corinne J. Naden.
p. cm.—(A gateway biography)
Includes index.
ISBN 0-7613-1805-4 (lib. bdg.)
1. Banneker, Benjamin, 1731–1806—Juvenile literature. 2. Astronomers—United States—Biography—Juvenile literature. 3. Afro-American scientists—United States—Biography—Juvenile literature. [1. Banneker, Benjamin, 1731–1806. 2. Astronomers. 3. Afro-Americans—Biography.] I. Naden, Corinne J. II. Series.
QB36.B22 B57 2001
520'.92—dc21
[B]   00-048208

Published by The Millbrook Press, Inc.
2 Old New Milford Road
Brookfield, Connecticut 06804
www.millbrookpress.com

Copyright © 2001 by Rose Blue and Corinne J. Naden
All rights reserved
Printed in the United States of America
5 4 3 2 1

BENJAMIN BANNEKER

Benjamin Banneker, 1731–1806

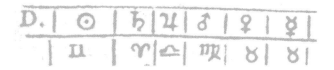

He was an astronomer, a mathematician, an inventor, and a writer. He published almanacs that listed daily sunrise and sunset. He built a wooden clock that kept perfect time and ran for fifty years. He helped to survey the land that became the new U.S. capital city of Washington, D.C. Yet, when Benjamin Banneker was born in 1731, not only was there no capital city, there was no United States.

Because Benjamin Banneker lived so long ago, there are no complete records about his life. But there are some things we know for sure. He never had much formal schooling. Mostly, he taught himself. In a time when slavery was part of America, this was quite remarkable. Benjamin Banneker was a black man, but not a slave. Most white people of the time thought they were superior to black people—whether they were a slave or not. Against the odds, this self-taught, gentle farmer of Maryland is remembered as America's first major black man of science.

Banneker's story doesn't begin in America, however. It begins across the sea in the south of England. It was the late seventeenth century. A cattle farmer claimed that his servant Molly Welsh stole a pail of milk. Young Molly said the cow kicked over the pail and spilled it. But the farmer didn't believe her story, so Molly was arrested.

That wasn't unusual. In those days, people were often arrested for small crimes. For more serious crimes such as stealing, sometimes the penalty was hanging! But England also had another way of dealing with criminals. If they weren't hanged, they might be sent overseas to the English colonies (which eventually became the United States). The colonies always needed more workers.

Molly Welsh was lucky. She escaped hanging because, of all things, she could read. Reading was important in the colonies. So, instead of being hanged, she was sent to a tobacco farm in the colony of Maryland. Molly arrived in the English colonies around 1683.

A tobacco plantation

After seven long years of hard work, Molly Welsh had her freedom. Now what? With no money and no family, what could she do in this new land? She rented a small farm several miles west of the city of Baltimore, Maryland. She planted tobacco and worked hard. In fact, she worked so hard that, in two or three years, she was able to buy her own small farm and two slaves.

One of the slaves was a charming man who said he was a prince from Senegal (a country in Africa). Indeed, he might have been. Sometimes African tribes captured members of other royal families and sold them into slavery. The slave's name was Bannaka, which was later changed to Banneky.

Around 1696, Molly Welsh gave both her slaves their freedom. Shortly after, she married Banneky. The marriage wasn't legal at the time, because Molly Welsh was a white woman. In Maryland in the late seventeenth century, if a white woman married a black man and had children, she lost her freedom. So the couple kept to themselves on their farm.

Their first child, Mary, was born in 1700. Three other daughters followed. This was an interesting family. Mother was a blue-eyed, blond-haired woman who told her children about English country life. Father was a dark-skinned African man, perhaps a prince, who spoke of ancient tribal customs. However, when he died at an early age, Molly was left to raise the children alone.

In 1730, daughter Mary married a man named Robert, from Guinea, West Africa. Robert took her last name. Some records say that Robert was a freed slave; others say that Mary bought Robert, freed him, and then married him, as her mother had bought, freed, and married Bannaka. To Molly's relief, Mary and Robert stayed on the farm.

In 1731, on November 9, Benjamin was born to Mary and Robert. Over the next several years they also had three girls. In time, the family name evolved into the spelling of Banneker.

Hardworking Robert saved enough money to buy his own farm near Molly's. To protect his family's rights, he drew up the deed in his name and that of his son.

There was very little schooling for black or white people in rural Baltimore County, Maryland. Luckily for Benjamin, his grandmother could read.

One of her proudest possessions was her Bible that she brought from England. She would tell her young grandson to "bring me the book," and the lessons would begin. Whenever Benjamin was not working in the tobacco fields, or weeding vegetables, or feeding the animals, he was at his grandmother's side, learning to read. And with a goose quill pen, Grandma Molly also taught her grandson to write.

It was clear to Molly that young Benjamin was very bright and eager to learn. He was interested in mathematics and could solve difficult problems. As soon as she taught him numbers, he went around the farm counting everything— caterpillars, twinkling stars in the night sky, kernels of new corn. "Benjie," said his grandmother, "I don't know what there is left for you to count." But there was always something.

When Benjamin Banneker was twelve years old, his grandmother knew he needed more schooling than she could give him. By that time, Peter Heinrich, a Quaker, had moved into the valley. Quakers belong to the religious group known as the Society of Friends. They are against slavery and believe that all people should be treated equally.

Peter Heinrich opened a one-room school for *all* boys, which actually meant both black and white. Girls were not formally educated until the end of the eighteenth century. This school was unusual for the time, and Banneker became one of two or three black students. His classmate and lifelong friend Jacob Hall, also a free black man, later said that Banneker seemed to be interested in nothing but books.

Quakers (shown here) belong to the religious group known as the Society of Friends.

For Banneker, a whole new world opened up in that one-room school. Soon he adopted Quaker ways of thinking and dressing. He spent just four years there, and only the winter months at that. The rest of the time he had to be on the farm. But in that short period, he tried to learn everything the schoolmaster could teach him.

One of his teaching tools was a hornbook, which is a square board with a piece of paper covered by a see-through piece of horn. Young Benjamin soon learned to read the words on the paper. He loved reading. Day and night, indoors

Benjamin Banneker learned to read on a hornbook like this one.

and outdoors, by the firelight or under the stars, his nose was in a book whenever he had a free moment. But even more than reading, Banneker loved mathematics. Heinrich allowed the boy to take home as many books as he wished. Most of them were math books. He enjoyed solving math problems in his few spare moments. Whenever he completed a problem, he ran to show his proud grandmother.

When his father's health began to fail, Banneker spent more and more time working the farm. And more and more time alone. However, he continued to educate himself by reading whatever he could. He made up his own math problems. He kept his counting skills sharp by figuring out his neighbors' profits and losses on their farms.

When Banneker was about twenty-one years old, he did something that made him quite famous in rural Maryland. He decided to build a clock. Banneker had never seen the inside of a clock, and he had no idea how a clock worked. He had seen a pocket watch, however. According to later reports, he borrowed a pocket watch to use as a model for his clock. It supposedly belonged to Josef Levi, a neighbor and friend.

It was no small thing to have a clock at this time in America. Telling time wasn't so easy or so important. Practically no one kept track of the time. It wasn't necessary. Farmers went out in the fields when the sun came up and came in when the sun went down. That was when meals were served. People went to bed after that.

It wouldn't have done any good for church bells to announce the time. Most plantations were so far from the church that the bells couldn't be heard anyway. If something really big happened, like the arrival of a ship from Europe, someone fired off a cannon.

Banneker was fascinated by the workings of the pocket watch. He took it apart, put it back together, and studied the movements of the second, minute, and hour wheels. Then he made drawings of his studies. Next, he used his math skills to enlarge the wheels to fit a clock. Then he selected the pieces of wood that he would use. Except for some iron and brass parts, the clock

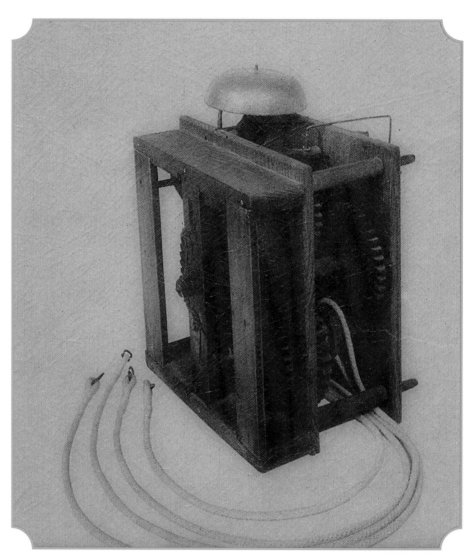

Amazingly, Banneker was able
to build a clock like this one by
studying the workings of a
pocket watch.

was made entirely of wood. For a final touch, he added a bell. Not only did his clock work, it chimed and kept perfect time for more than fifty years.

The young man was pleased with his clock making, but his neighbors were astounded! Banneker's was not the first clock built in the colonies, but the others were usually made in the large cities by professional craftsmen. The fact that Banneker was a twenty-two-year-old farmer, who had probably never seen a book on clock making, made his clock even more incredible.

In 1759, about six years after the clock making, Banneker's father died, leaving the farm to him. Banneker's three sisters had already married and were living in the area. Now, Banneker was busier than ever. The entire farm was his responsibility. According to records, he was a successful farmer. In his spare time, he learned to play the flute and the violin, and in 1763, at the age of thirty-two, he bought his first book. It was a Bible.

Banneker and his mother lived alone on the farm for many years. The story goes that, at the age of twenty-seven, he fell in love with a woman named Anola. Anola was a slave on a neighboring

Banneker's father wrote up this deed,
or contract, which legally left the farm
to Banneker.

plantation. When her owner would not sell her, Banneker planned to steal her away and sail to England where they could be married. But the plan failed, and Anola drowned herself in despair. Banneker never married.

It was a lonely life for a free black man. Banneker's neighbors respected him as a person of learning and skill, but in that time, they could never be true friends. Life could have continued at this pace, and nothing more could have been heard of this remarkable man of science. But one day in 1771, new neighbors bought some land on the Patapsco River not far from Banneker's farm. They changed the life of this brilliant, quiet, and lonely man.

Andrew Ellicott II had come to America from England in the early 1700s, settling in Pennsylvania. He married and had five sons. When Andrew died, his oldest son, Joseph, was running a successful gristmill. A gristmill is a mill that grinds grain for customers.

In 1766, Joseph was left a lot of money by a relative in Ireland. He and his brothers bought 700 acres (283 hectares) of land to make a new mill along the Patapsco River about 10 miles (16 kilometers) from Baltimore. The city of Baltimore was now the most populated area in Maryland.

In 1771, the Ellicotts began work on their new mill. By the time it opened in 1774, Banneker was a constant visitor. He was fascinated with the mill's workings and would often ask the workmen to show him how the machines worked. Banneker also noticed that the Ellicotts used no slaves at the mill, even though it was legal.

About half of Maryland's white families at the time owned at least one slave. But the Ellicotts were different. They were Quakers. Besides providing work for people in the area, they also bought food supplies from Banneker's farm. In time, Banneker mostly grew grain, which he sold to the Ellicott mill.

Banneker became good friends with the Ellicotts. Joseph, who was also a clock maker, heard about Banneker's famous chiming clock. He invited Banneker to see his own creation, a clock 8 feet (2.4 meters) tall with four faces. But it was George Ellicott who really changed Banneker's life.

George was Joseph's nephew and twenty-nine years younger than Banneker. George was given the job of surveying, or measuring, land for a road from the mill to Baltimore. A trained surveyor since the age of sixteen, George made maps and directed the workers, sometimes while Banneker watched. Before long the two became friends. George would often visit the Banneker farm to discuss machines and other topics. The young man also loaned Banneker some tools and books on different subjects.

It was now 1788. The American Revolution had ended five years earlier. Maryland became the seventh state to join the new United States of America. Like other farmers in the area,

Banneker had grown food to help feed George Washington's army. Now fifty-seven years old, Banneker was alone on the farm; his mother had died a few years earlier. But he had his friends the Ellicotts, and he had his work.

Banneker's work included a new interest in astronomy. George Ellicott had loaned him some books and a telescope. A self-taught stargazer, Banneker began to figure out when there would be a solar eclipse in the area. Predicting a solar eclipse is not easy. He had to chart the paths of the sun and the moon.

A solar eclipse occurs when the moon passes between the sun and the earth. The moon makes a shadow on the earth's surface. From earth, it looks like the moon is blocking out the sun's light.

A total eclipse happens only about every 360 years in the same place. Many partial solar eclipses may occur each year. In ancient times, some peoples believed that, during a solar eclipse, a dragon was eating the sun. Others thought that the gods were displeased or that devils and witches were to blame.

Banneker's interest in astronomy now led him into a new field. In the fall of 1790, he told George Ellicott that he had completed his first almanac,

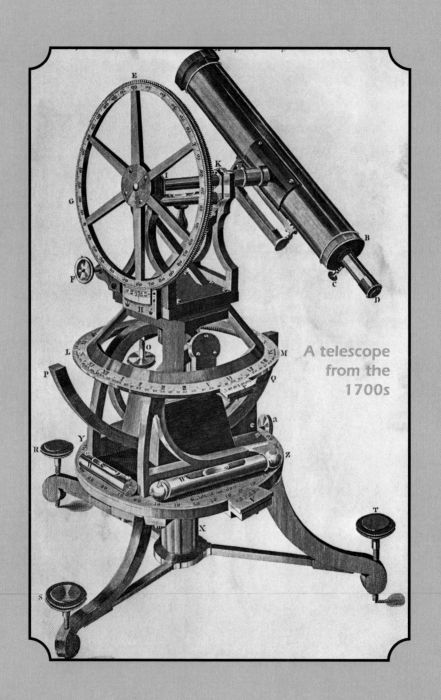

A telescope from the 1700s

which included his eclipse predictions. George was amazed.

If a home held only two books in eighteenth-century America, they were surely the Bible and an almanac. Benjamin Franklin had been publishing his *Poor Richard's Almanack* since 1732, and it was still very popular. An almanac was the household dictionary and reference book. No matter how many were published, there was always room for one more.

Anyone who could read certainly read the almanac. It told the times of sunrise and sunset. It told farmers the best time to plant crops and harvest them. It told fishers when the tides would come in and go out. It gave sailors the positions of the moon and stars for navigation. It told families what holidays were coming up so they could plan their festive meals.

It also included a table, called an ephemeris, showing the positions of the sun, moon, and planets for each day of the year. Banneker was especially interested in that. And he was especially interested in publishing a farmer's almanac because it focused on farm issues. The most famous of these publications is called sim-

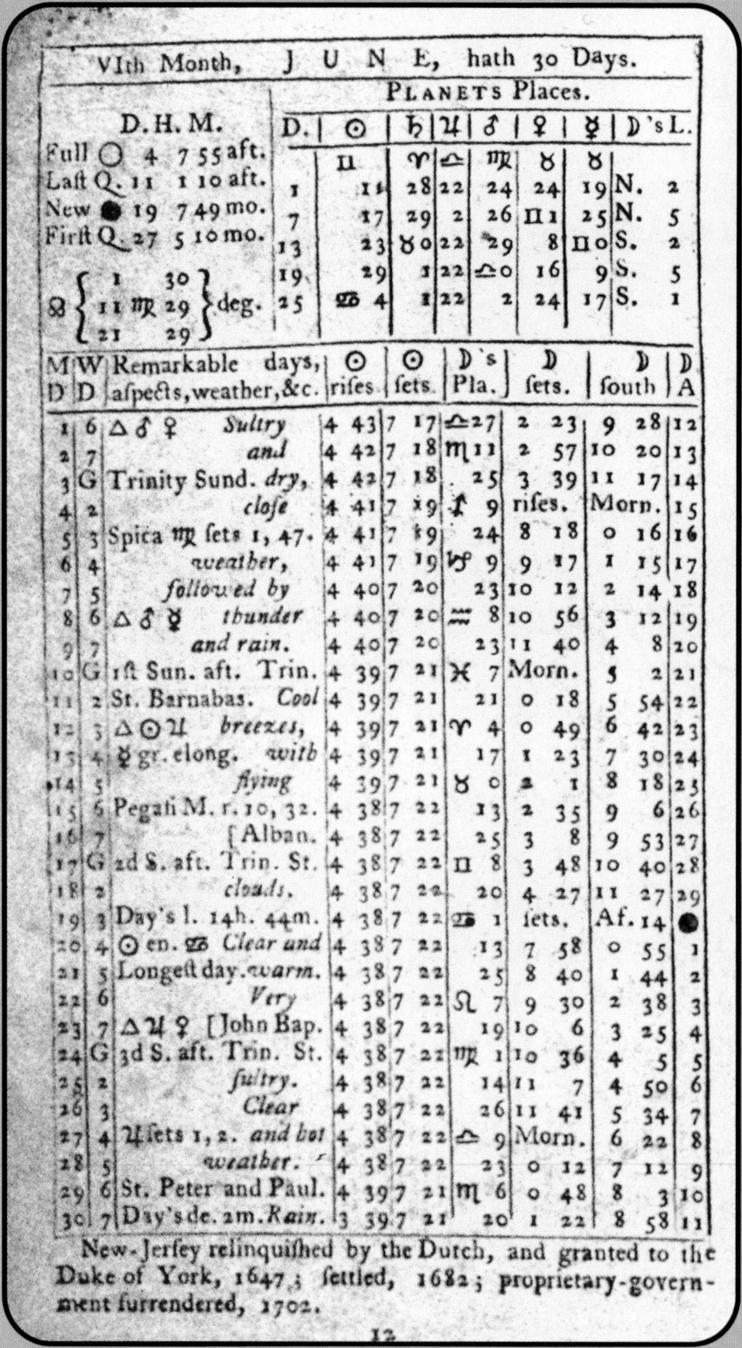

VIth Month, J U N E, hath 30 Days.

D. H. M.			
Full ○	4	7 55	aft.
Laſt Q.	11	1 10	aft.
New ●	19	7 49	mo.
Firſt Q.	27	5 10	mo.

☊ { 1 30 / 11 ♍ 29 / 21 29 } deg.

PLANETS Places.

D.	☉	♄	♃	♂	♀	☿	☽'s L.
	♊	♈	♎	♍	♉	♉	
1	11	28	22	24	24	19	N. 2
7	17	29	2	26	♊ 1	25	N. 5
13	23	♉ 0	22	29	8	♊ 0	S. 2
19	29	1	22	♎ 0	16	9	S. 5
25	♋ 4	1	22	2	24	17	S. 1

M D	W D	Remarkable days, aſpects, weather, &c.	☉ rises	☉ ſets.	☽'s Pla.	☽ ſets.	☽ ſouth	☽ A
1	6	△ ♂ ♀ *Sultry*	4 43	7 17	♎ 27	2 23	9 28	12
2	7	*and*	4 42	7 18	♏ 11	2 57	10 20	13
3	G	Trinity Sund. *dry,*	4 42	7 18	25	3 39	11 17	14
4	2	*cloſe*	4 41	7 19	♐ 9	riſes.	Morn.	15
5	3	Spica ♍ ſets 1, 47.	4 41	7 19	24	8 18	0 16	16
6	4	*weather,*	4 41	7 19	♑ 9	9 17	1 15	17
7	5	*followed by*	4 40	7 20	23	10 12	2 14	18
8	6	△ ♂ ☿ *thunder*	4 40	7 20	♒ 8	10 56	3 12	19
9	7	*and rain.*	4 40	7 20	23	11 40	4 8	20
10	G	1ſt Sun. aft. Trin.	4 39	7 21	♓ 7	Morn.	5 2	21
11	2	St. Barnabas. *Cool*	4 39	7 21	21	0 18	5 54	22
12	3	△ ☉ ♃ *breezes,*	4 39	7 21	♈ 4	0 49	6 42	23
13	4	☿ gr. elong. *with*	4 39	7 21	17	1 23	7 30	24
14	5	*flying*	4 39	7 21	♉ 0	2 1	8 18	25
15	6	Pegaſi M. r. 10, 32.	4 38	7 22	13	2 35	9 6	26
16	7	[Alban.	4 38	7 22	25	3 8	9 53	27
17	G	2d S. aft. Trin. St.	4 38	7 22	♊ 8	3 48	10 40	28
18	2	*clouds.*	4 38	7 22	20	4 27	11 27	29
19	3	Day's l. 14h. 44m.	4 38	7 22	♋ 1	ſets.	Af. 14	●
20	4	☉ en. ♋ *Clear and*	4 38	7 22	13	7 58	0 55	1
21	5	Longeſt day. *warm.*	4 38	7 22	25	8 40	1 44	2
22	6	*Very*	4 38	7 22	♌ 7	9 30	2 38	3
23	7	△ ♃ ♀ [John Bap.	4 38	7 22	19	10 6	3 25	4
24	G	3d S. aft. Trin. St.	4 38	7 22	♍ 1	10 36	4 5	5
25	2	*ſultry.*	4 38	7 22	14	11 7	4 50	6
26	3	*Clear*	4 38	7 22	26	11 41	5 34	7
27	4	♃ ſets 1, 2. *and hot*	4 38	7 22	♎ 9	Morn.	6 22	8
28	5	*weather.*	4 38	7 22	23	0 12	7 12	9
29	6	St. Peter and Paul.	4 39	7 21	♏ 6	0 48	8 3	10
30	7	Day's de. 2m. *Rain.*	3 39	7 21	20	1 22	8 58	11

New-Jerſey relinquiſhed by the Dutch, and granted to the Duke of York, 1647; ſettled, 1682; proprietary-government ſurrendered, 1702.

12

This is an example of an ephemeris, which is a table used in astronomy that shows the position of the sun, moon, and planets for each day of the year.

ply *The Farmer's Almanac*, and it is still published today.

An almanac is not easy to prepare. It takes a great knowledge of astronomy. For nearly a year, Banneker gained that knowledge. Astronomy became his great and lasting interest. He watched the night sky and studied the cycles of the moon. His almanac included the time eclipses would happen, the time the sun and moon would rise and set, when rain and droughts might happen, and a table showing the tides for Chesapeake Bay.

When his almanac was finished, a proud Benjamin Banneker sent his work to Baltimore's most important publisher, Goddard & Angell. Then he learned a lesson that many authors learn. Goddard & Angell didn't want his almanac. The next two publishers he sent it to didn't want it either.

Banneker knew this could be the first almanac published by a black man. Did the white publishers believe an African American could not create such work? Banneker turned to George Ellicott for help. But it was George's cousin, Andrew Ellicott IV, who helped this time. He contacted his friend James Pemberton, president of the Pennsylvania Society for the Abolition of Slavery.

The cover of the
1833 Farmers' Almanac,
which is the most popular
almanac available that
focuses on farm issues

Wouldn't the society be interested in helping publish an almanac by a black man?

In 1791, while Banneker waited for news on his almanac, he became involved in what he thought of as his life's great adventure. He was sixty years old and had never been more than a dozen miles from home. The newly formed United States of America needed a capital city. Northern and southern states could not agree on a site, so they left it up to the president.

President George Washington chose a commission to take a survey, or measure the land, of 10 square miles (26 square kilometers) on the Potomac River. This land was donated by the states of Maryland and Virginia. It was a good location. George Washington himself was a trained surveyor, but since he had other matters to attend to, he appointed Andrew Ellicott IV to be in charge of the team.

Ellicott was told to gather a crew and begin the work immediately. He wrote to his cousin George, also a surveyor. But George was busy and could not be away for such a long time. George, however, suggested Banneker instead. Andrew agreed. Some historians believe that it was Thomas Jefferson who suggested Banneker.

George Washington chose Andrew Ellicott to be in charge of the team that surveyed the land along the Potomac River.

Banneker and Ellicott traveled on horseback to Alexandria, Virginia. They set up camp in the wilderness on the bank of the Potomac River. First, they put up an observation tent on the highest spot they could find. Then they cut a hole in the top for a telescope.

Banneker spent a lot of time in the observation tent, leaving the physical outside jobs to younger men. He watched the astronomical clock, which kept the exact time of all telescope sightings. He studied the positions of the stars to measure positions on land. He also kept careful notes of all calculations and instrument readings. During the beginning months of surveying, George Washington visited the site. It is likely that Banneker met the president at that time.

Even though most of his work was inside the tent, the weather was hard on Banneker's health.

He stayed with the sur-
vey team for three
months. By then, the
four corners of the new
city had been determined
and marked. Although
there was much more
work still to be done,
Banneker was worried
about planting season.
He had asked his sisters
to look after the farm in
his absence, but he felt
he could not be away any
longer. So, in April 1791,
he returned to his farm and his almanac.

Banneker used this instrument, which belonged to Andrew Ellicott, while surveying the land. It is called a zenith sector.

In the meantime, James Pemberton of the Pennsylvania Society for the Abolition of Slavery had contacted Joseph Townsend, president of the Maryland Society for Promoting the Abolition of Slavery. First, they checked to see if Banneker was actually a skilled astronomer. Elias Ellicott, one of George Ellicott's brothers, assured the men that he was. Pemberton and Townsend agreed to find a publisher. They realized that an almanac by

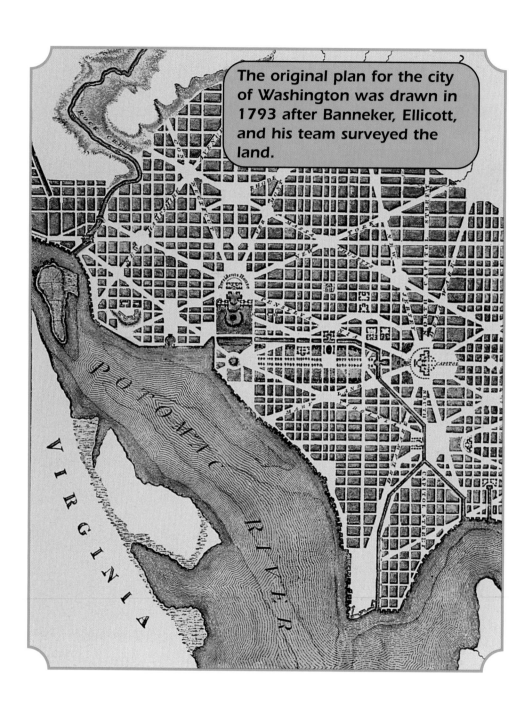

an African American would be important to their cause.

After his return from the survey site, Banneker worked until June on his table of calculations for the eclipses. They were included in his first almanac, published in 1791.

Banneker became something of a celebrity. Members of abolition societies promoted his achievement, stressing that Banneker was a black man. People who were against slavery used his work as proof that the black race was not inferior to the white race. Banneker might have preferred that his work be judged on its merits alone, but for now it was enough that it was published.

Around the time of the publication of the first almanac, Banneker did an extraordinary thing. On August 19, 1791, he wrote a letter to Thomas Jefferson, who was secretary of state to George Washington. Jefferson later became the third president of the United States.

Banneker included in his letter a copy of his eclipse tables. He wrote about both men's long-standing interest in science. The letter also attacked slavery and indirectly asked for a reply. It commented on the condition of blacks in America and compared it to slavery in the British colonies. He recalled Jefferson's own elegant words as the author of the Declaration of Independence: "We hold these truths to be self-evident, that all men are created equal...." Banneker asked Jefferson "and all others" to put aside any prejudices and, instead, to fill their hearts with kindness toward the enslaved people.

Jefferson was highly respected. But his position on slavery was often questionable. Although he claimed that "all men are created equal," Jefferson owned slaves himself. He said he defended slavery because it was the will of the people he represented in government. But, in his own will, he didn't free his own slaves.

Banneker's letter is extraordinary because it is a bold move for this gentle man. According to the records, he never voiced opinions about slavery. Yet it seems reasonable that he would have had strong feelings on the subject because of his parents and grandparents. On his isolated Maryland farm, he may have had little contact with slaves, but he knew that slavery existed all around him.

Jefferson answered Banneker's letter four days after receiving it. The abolitionists were very happy with this publicity for their cause. Jefferson's reply was short but sympathetic. He

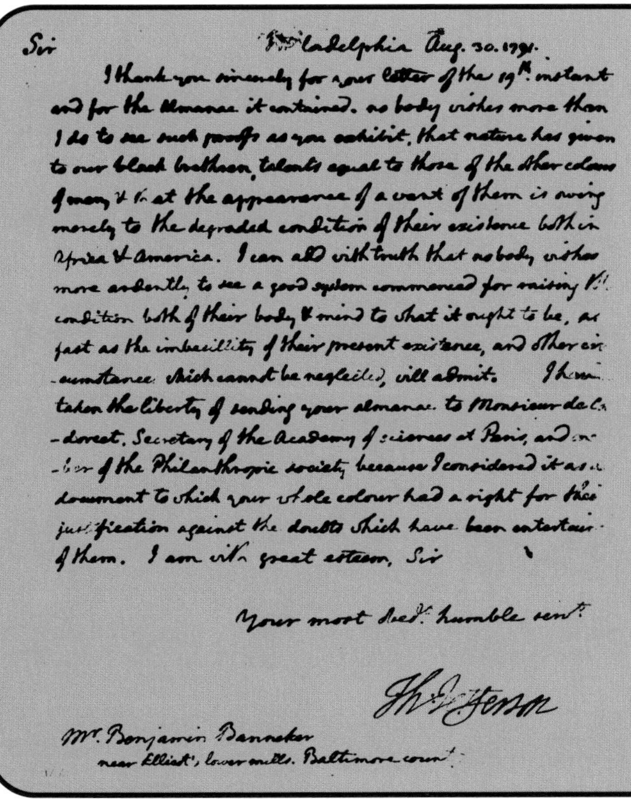

Sir — Philadelphia Aug. 30. 1791.

I thank you sincerely for your letter of the 19th instant and for the Almanac it contained. no body wishes more than I do to see such proofs as you exhibit, that nature has given to our black brethren, talents equal to those of the other colours of men, & that the appearance of a want of them is owing merely to the degraded condition of their existence both in Africa & America. I can add with truth that no body wishes more ardently to see a good system commenced for raising the condition both of their body & mind to what it ought to be, as fast as the imbecillity of their present existence, and other circumstance which cannot be neglected, will admit. I have taken the liberty of sending your almanac to Monsieur de Condorcet, Secretary of the Academy of sciences at Paris, and member of the Philanthropic society because I considered it as a document to which your whole colour had a right for their justification against the doubts which have been entertained of them. I am with great esteem, Sir

Your most obedt. humble servt.

Th: Jefferson

Mr. Benjamin Banneker
near Ellicot's lower mills. Baltimore county.

Thomas Jefferson wrote this letter to Benjamin Banneker on August 30, 1791.

said, "No body wishes more than I do to see such proofs as you exhibit, that nature has given to our black brethren talents equal to that of other colors of men."

Jefferson added that he hoped for a new system that would improve the "state of the Negro" in America. He also told Banneker that he had sent a copy of the almanac to a friend, the secretary of the Royal Academy of Sciences in Paris, France.

He did so, said Jefferson, to show "the equal talents of the Negro race."

In December 1791, Banneker's first almanac went on sale. It was entitled *Benjamin Banneker's Pennsylvania, Delaware, Maryland and Virginia Almanac and Ephemeris for the Year of Our Lord,*

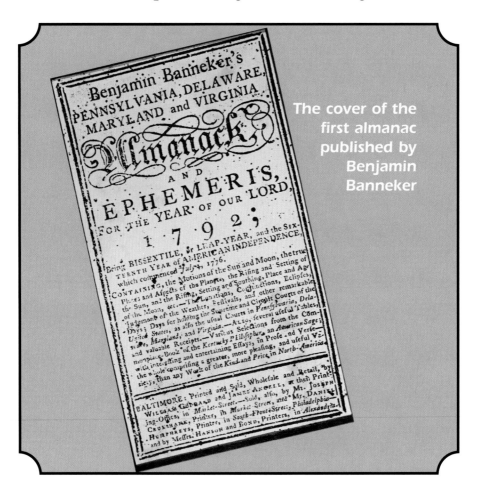

The cover of the first almanac published by Benjamin Banneker

1792. Goddard & Angell, who had once rejected the work, had agreed to publish it, no doubt because of the abolitionist societies of Pennsylvania and Maryland. The publishers were not shy about advertising the author's race. The title page read: "The Editors . . . feel themselves gratified in the Opportunity of presenting to the Public . . . what must be considered an extraordinary Effort of Genius . . . calculated by a sable Descendant of Africa . . . "

Whether because of all the advertising, Banneker's excellent work, or both, the first almanac sold very well. Banneker was astonished. He was even more astonished by his sudden fame. Used to living alone, he was now often visited by neighbors and strangers who had read his almanac and heard of his chiming clock. He invited them in and enjoyed the attention.

Banneker, however, did not have a lot of free time for visitors. As soon as his first almanac went on sale, he became busy preparing tables for the second one. Now he even had a second publisher. Joseph Crukshank of Philadelphia agreed to publish the 1793 edition, as did Angell, who had ended the partnership with Goddard.

The second almanac contained the same information as did the first, and it included more stories and essays. It also contained a copy, without editorial comment, of the reply by Thomas Jefferson to Banneker's letter criticizing slavery.

Another feature in the 1793 almanac proposed a unique plan. The proposal introduced "A Plan Of a Peace Office for the United States." It suggested a new office for the federal government to be headed by a secretary of peace. At the time, there was a War Department headed by a secretary of war.

For some time, this idea of a peace office was thought to be the work of Benjamin Banneker, who was strongly against war and slavery. But now the suggestion is attributed to Dr. Benjamin Rush of Philadelphia, who was also against slavery and war.

Today, the U.S. Cabinet is made up of fourteen major executive departments of government, including State (established in 1789), Defense (1947, including the War Department, which was created in 1789), Transportation (1966), and Veterans Affairs (1989). But there is still no secretary of peace.

If Benjamin Banneker could have seen a news-paper headline or heard a news broadcast on January 1, 1793, he would have felt a sense of pride. On that day, the survey for the City of Washington, District of Columbia, was completed. In September, George Washington himself laid the cornerstone for the Capitol, where Congress would meet.

After 1793, Banneker published five more almanacs, the last one in 1797. His best-selling year was 1794. The 1795 edition showed his pic-

This picture of Banneker was printed on the cover of his 1795 almanac—his name was changed later to the spelling we use today.

ture on the cover. He is dressed in a style typical for a man during the eighteenth century—jacket, waistcoat, shirt, and neckcloth.

After the 1795 edition, sales began to decline. More and more almanacs were being published, and a black author was no longer a big selling point. Americans were not as enthusiastic about the abolitionist movement. Most of them believed that slavery was a local issue. This feeling remained until the 1860s, when the fight over slavery was resolved by the American Civil War.

While he was busy with his almanacs, Banneker had little time to grow tobacco. Perhaps it was time to quit farming. He kept a small plot for his vegetable garden and rented out the rest of his land to neighbors. But Banneker was not a very good landlord. He was shy about collecting overdue rents, and he became upset about arguments over money.

Maybe it was time to sell the farm. This was a hard decision because the land had been in his family for many years. But it was made easier by selling the farm to the Ellicotts. They paid him a fair price, assuring him a yearly income for as long as he lived. In addition, he could live on the farm as long as he wished.

Without the farm, Banneker was free to pursue his interests in astronomy and mathematics. He would often sit each night studying the sky through his telescope. He also spent a good deal of time at the Ellicott's store.

So the years passed until 1806. On Sunday, October 9, one month before his seventy-fifth birthday, Banneker took his usual morning walk. Suddenly, he felt ill. A neighbor helped him back to his cabin. He died that afternoon.

Two days later, during his burial service on the farm, a very strange thing happened. In full sight of everyone there, Banneker's wooden cabin suddenly caught fire. It burned to the ground. Nothing inside was saved, including his famous chiming clock.

Banneker was buried beneath a tulip tree on the land he loved. He left his few possessions to his sisters, except his worktable, telescopes, and other instruments. Those, along with his journals, went to his friend George Ellicott. Luckily, these items had been removed before the fire.

The Baltimore *Federal Gazette* wrote a modest obituary about this modest man. It ended with these words: "Mr. Banneker is a prominent instance to prove that a descendant of Africa is susceptible of as great mental improvement and deep knowledge into the mysteries of nature as that of any other nation."

During his lifetime, Banneker was always grateful for the help and friendship of the Ellicott family. After his death, they continued to help by recording most of the facts that we now know about Banneker's life. Martha Ellicott Tyson, daughter of George, was born in 1795 and was only eleven years old when Banneker died. But she heard, and later recorded, the many stories about him discussed by her father and relatives.

Martha Ellicott Tyson's short biography of Banneker, entitled *A Sketch*, was published for the Maryland Historical Society in the late 1840s. In it, Tyson said of Banneker: "He appears to have been the pioneer in the movement in this part of the world, toward the improvement of his race . . . and had already earned himself a respectable position amongst men of science."

Actually, Benjamin Banneker played a very slight role in the abolitionist movement. Certainly, he was eloquent in his words against slavery in the letter to Jefferson. But Banneker himself was a man who avoided confrontation of any sort. It is probable that he would not have written that letter without the urging of the abolition societies.

oday his country still remembers Benjamin Banneker and his achievements. Although his farm in rural Maryland is now a street near the town of Oella, a nearby marker honors him. It says: "Benjamin Banneker, 1731–1806, self-educated Negro mathematician-astronomer. He made the first Maryland Almanac in 1792. Assisted in survey of District of Columbia. His achievements recognized by Thomas Jefferson. Was born, lived his entire life and died near here."

On February 1, 1980, the U.S. Postal Service issued a stamp honoring Benjamin Banneker. The Maryland Historical Society also has many of the

This postage stamp was issued by the U.S. Postal Service in honor of Benjamin Banneker and his achievements.

scientific materials that Banneker left to the Ellicott family, as well as copies of his almanacs and letters. In England, his name has been placed in the records of Parliament.

Annapolis, Maryland, has a museum that honors both Benjamin Banneker and Frederick Douglass, the famed African American abolitionist of the nineteenth century. At one time, a school in the Catonsville, Maryland, area was named for Banneker as well. However, since it was for black students, it was closed in 1965 when segregated schools were banned. There is

Benjamin Banneker Park in Washington, D.C.

no longer a Banneker school, but there is a Banneker Circle in Washington, D.C. It adjoins L'Enfant Plaza, named for the Frenchman Pierre-Charles L'Enfant. L'Enfant designed the plan for the nation's capital by using the land survey Banneker helped to complete.

Although Banneker's home has not been reconstructed, the Benjamin Banneker Historical Park and Museum now occupies part of the farm site in Oella, Maryland. This is perhaps the remembrance that Banneker would have liked best of all. It displays historical and scientific arti-

The Benjamin Banneker Historical Park and Museum in Oella, Maryland, displays items related to Banneker's life.

facts of the time. In addition to the cheerful park, it provides families with a day of learning and fun. Children enjoy the surroundings as they learn more about this quiet man and the science of astronomy, which he so loved.

People still study the skies with as much curiosity as Banneker did on his Maryland farm two centuries earlier. Today, however, they have much better instruments than Banneker did. In 2000, the American Museum of Natural History in New York City opened its Rose Center for Earth and Space. With its fantastic displays and scientific instruments, it is dedicated to the exploration of the universe, its solar systems, and its galaxies. In some way, this twenty-first century marvel honors all dedicated star searchers, including Benjamin Banneker, the modest, unassuming pioneer who was America's first black man of science.

TIMELINE

About 1683   Accused of stealing milk, Molly Welsh is sent to America to work as a servant for seven years.

About 1689   Now free, Molly Welsh begins farming tobacco in Baltimore County.

About 1692   Welsh buys two slaves, one from Senegal named Bannaka.

About 1696   Welsh frees her slaves and marries Bannaka.

1700   Mary, Benjamin Banneker's mother, is born to Molly and Bannaka.

1730   Mary marries Robert, a free black, who takes her name.

1731   Benjamin is born, November 9, to Mary and Robert; surname is later changed to Banneker.

About 1743   Benjamin Banneker goes to a Quaker all boys school.

About 1753   Banneker constructs a chiming clock.

1759   Benjamin Banneker's father dies; Benjamin takes over the farm.

About 1790	Banneker predicts the solar eclipse.
1791	Banneker joins Washington, D.C., survey team; returns to his farm in April; writes a letter to Thomas Jefferson condemning slavery on August 19; his first almanac on sale in December.
1793	Washington, D.C., survey completed.
1797	Banneker's last almanac is published.
1800	President John Adams moves into the White House; federal government moves into Washington, D.C.
1806	Banneker dies at home on October 9. During burial services on October 11, his farm mysteriously burns to the ground.

FOR MORE INFORMATION

Books

Hinman, Bonnie, and Arthur M. Schlesinger. *Benjamin Banneker: American Mathematician and Astronomer.* Broomall, Pa: Chelsea House, 2000.

Litwin, Laura Baskes. *Benjamin Banneker: Astronomer and Mathematician.* Springfield, N.J.: Enslow, 1999.

Maupin, Melissa. *Benjamin Banneker: Journey to Freedom.* Chanhassen, Minn.: The Child's World, 1999.

McGill, Alice, and Chris K. Soentpiet. *Molly Bannaky.* Boston, Mass.: Houghton Mifflin, 1999.

Web Sites

Banneker–Douglass Museum
http://www.marylandhistoricaltrust.net/bdm.html

Benjamin Banneker, Letter to Thomas Jefferson
http://longman.awl.com/nash/primarysource_6_3.htm

Black History Month: A Celebration
http://www.kron.com/specials/blackhistory/home.html

The Black Inventor Online Museum
http://www.blackinventor.com

INDEX